이 시집은 누군가의
마음 문 앞에서 두드리는
소리없는 노크입니다

감사합니다

2025년 여름

저자

이 원로 드림

Lee Won-Ro's 61st Poetry Collection

이원로 61번째 시집

Silent Knocks
소리 없는 노크

시산맥 기획시선 148

Silent Knocks
소리 없는 노크

시산맥 기획시선 148

초판 1쇄 인쇄 | 2025년 5월 25일
초판 1쇄 발행 | 2025년 5월 30일

지은이 이원로
펴낸이 문정영
펴낸곳 시산맥사
편집주간 김필영
편집위원 최연수 박민서
등록번호 제300-2013-12호
등록일자 2009년 4월 15일
주소 03131 서울특별시 종로구 율곡로 6길 36. 월드오피스텔 1102호
전화 02-764-8722, 010-8894-8722
전자우편 poemmtss@naver.com
시산맥카페 http://cafe.daum.net/poemmtss

ISBN 979-11-6243-591-5 (03810) 종이책
ISBN 979-11-6243-592-2 (05810) 전자책

값 12,000원

* 이 책은 전부 또는 일부 내용을 재사용하려면 반드시 저작권자와 시산맥사의 동의를 받아야 합니다.
* 이 책은 교보문고와 연계하여 전자북으로 발간되었습니다.
* 본문 페이지에서 한 연이 첫 번째 행에서 시작될 때에는 〈 표기를 합니다.
* 저자의 의도에 따라 작품의 보조 동사와 합성 명사는 띄어쓰기가 달라질 수 있습니다.

Lee Won-Ro's 61st Poetry Collection

이원로 61번째 시집

Silent Knocks

소리 없는 노크

Lee Won-Ro 이원로

| Prologue |

Joy

A fleeting smile,Rippling joy.

Is it the joy of harvest,Or the smile of conquest?

Could it be the sacred joy,Born of holy zeal?

Or the sensual joy,Kindled by primal passion?

Clearly a beast in form,
Yet adorned with angel's wings.

기쁨

스쳐 가는 미소
물결치는 기쁨

추수의 기쁨인지
정복의 미소인지

성스러운 열의가 이룬
거룩한 기쁨일지

본능의 열정이 해낸
관능의 기쁨일지

분명 짐승 모습인데
천사 날개가 달렸지

■ 차례

Part I Emanation
제1부 발산

Bulbs 구근	19
Winter Sky 겨울 하늘	21
How Regrettable 안타까워	23
Before the Day Ends 저물기 전	25
Grumbling 투정	27
Oneness 일체	29
Threads 실오라기	31
Grace Period 유예기간	33
Vestigial Eyes 흔적 눈	35
Emanation 발산	37
Escape 탈출	39

Part II The Wind Always Blows
제2부 바람은 언제나 분다

The Wind Always Blows 바람은 언제나 분다	43
Attraction 끌림	45
Daydream 백일몽	47
Insight 혜안	49
Prescription 처방	51
Despair 낙망	53
The Hidden Stream 숨어 흐르는 강물	55
Wounds 상처	57
Winter Riverside 겨울 강가	59
Drawing Lots 제비뽑기	61
A Striking Sensation 강렬한 느낌	63

Part III The Drummer
제3부 북 치는 사람

The Drummer 북 치는 사람	67
An Immortal Glimpse 불후의 일별	69
A Cozy Night 포근한 밤	71
Nostalgia 향수	73
The Elevator 승강기	75
The Fox and the Bear 여우와 곰	77
Illiteracy and Ignorance 문맹과 무지	79
Disposal 처분	81
Consideration 배려	83
The Final Gaze 마지막 시선	85
Doubt and Worry 의심과 걱정	87

Part IV Smile
제4부 미소

The Wheel 바퀴	91
Sprouting Shoots 돋아나는 싹	93
Judgment Day 심판의 날	95
Spacefaring 우주여행	97
The Root of Supplication 간구의 뿌리	99
How Fragile We Are 얼마나 허약한지	101
Joy and Comfort 기쁨과 위로	103
The Face of the Winter Solstice 동지의 얼굴	105
Mother's Eyes 엄마 눈	107
The Square Jungle 사각의 정글	109
Smile 미소	111

Part V Order
제5부 질서

Reemergence 재현	115
Paradox 역설	117
Waste 낭비	119
Feed 모이	121
The Bond 끈	123
A Hint 귀띔	125
A Mark 징표	127
Witch Hunt 마녀사냥	129
Archaeologist 고고학자	131
Counterattack 응전	133
Order 질서	135

Part I
Emanation

제1부
발산

Bulbs

Clearing the riverside reed fields,
I carefully plant the bulbs in place.

Covered by a cozy blanket of snow,
They slumber through the snug winter,
Dreaming of great hopes
To bloom anew in the spring.

Though what is planted may sprout,
Flowers bloom, and fruits ripen,
Who can guarantee
How they will bloom or what they will bear
Until the moment is revealed?

Even with tender care and devotion,
The fruits will not follow one's desires.
May it not lead to the lament of ignorance,
But to the joy of wisdom instead.

May the heart that plants these bulbs
Not be a plea without assurance.

구근

냇가 갈대밭을 파내고
구근을 가지런히 심는다

포근한 눈 이불 덮고
아늑한 겨울잠 자며
대망의 꿈을 꾸어
새봄을 피어내려 서리

심은 대로 싹이 트고
꽃 피어 열매 맺는다지만
어찌 피어 무얼 맺을지
볼 때까지 장담 못 하리

애지중지 키워내도
열매는 마음대로 아니리
탄식하는 우매가 아니라
기뻐하는 지혜를 받게 되길

구근을 심는 마음이
보장 없는 간구 아니길

Winter Sky

Stripped of all their leaves,
The trees by the stream
Sway in the early winter breeze.

Someone says, "Lift your eyes and look."
In the winter sky, heralding the season,
What signals will each of them receive?

Amid the biting cold and blizzards,
A fierce game of survival unfolds,
Fighting to preserve life.

Even as hearts grow cold,
Dreams of living remain,
And survival endures.

Dreams arise from the body,
And dreams sustain the body.
How could the two ever be separated?

겨울 하늘

잎새를 몽땅 털어버리고
초겨울 바람에 흔들리는
시냇가 나무들이 보이리

누군가 눈을 들어 바라보란다
때를 알리는 겨울 하늘에서
무슨 신호를 각자 받게 될지

한파와 눈보라 속에
생명을 지켜 나가려는
생존 게임이 치열하리

심장을 얼려가면서도
생활의 꿈이 있기에
생존이 버텨나가리

몸에서 꿈이 나오고
꿈이 몸을 살려가지
어찌 둘을 따로 가르리

How Regrettable

Immersed in true joy,
Laughing gleefully like an infant.

In that moment, without realizing,
All obstacles fade away.

Amidst the wondrous light,
Freedom is fully embraced.

How regrettable,
Truly regrettable.

That such a state of bliss
Can only last for a fleeting moment.

Is there anyone who could
Stretch this moment longer,
Much, much longer?

안타까워

진정한 기쁨에 잠겨
갓난애처럼 깔깔 웃지

저도 모르게 그 순간
장애물이 다 걷히리

놀라운 빛 가운데
자유를 만끽하리

안타까워
정녕 안타까워

이런 경지가 오직
순간에만 머물다니

누가 있어 이 순간을
길게 길게 늘여 주지

Before the Day Ends

Every minute, every second is precious time,
A treasured gift inviting you to savor it.

While you can see,
While you can hear,
While you can eat,
While you can move,

Before the day comes to an end,
Freely, while you can feel, as your heart desires.

What does it mean
To truly live to your fullest?
What will I choose to do,
Freely, as my heart desires?

저물기 전

매분 매초는 진귀한 시간
만끽해 보라는 귀중한 선물

볼 수 있을 때
들을 수 있는 동안
먹을 수 있을 때
움직일 수 있는 동안

날이 저물기 전에 마음껏
느낄 수 있을 때 생각대로

어찌하는 게
너의 마음껏 인가
생각대로 나는
무엇을 할 건지

Grumbling

Under the dazzling sky,
Amid rays of light carried by the wind,
Lively leaves sway,
Engaged in an endless dance.

They stand, holding more light
Than darkness within,
Shaking off sadness,
And embracing comfort instead.

Flowing water, drifting clouds, and the wind,
Migratory birds searching for food,
Countless stars in the sky and flowers on the earth—
Do any of them ever grumble?

투정

눈부신 하늘 아래
바람에 실린 빛살 속에
발랄한 잎새들이
그침 없는 무도 중이지

어둠보다는 빛을
많이 품어서지
슬픔은 털어내고
위로를 간직해서지

흐르는 물과 구름과 바람
먹이 찾아 헤매는 철새
무수한 하늘의 별 땅의 꽃
누구 하나 투정하든가

Oneness

The body and mind are one,
Laughing and crying in sync,
Shrinking and trembling together.

An endless network of circuits,
Countless wireless signals,
Tightly interwoven as one.

Though they endlessly clash,
Bound by an unbreakable loop,
They find resolution in harmony and compromise.

Even until the moment of farewell,
The conflict never truly ends,
And yet, one remains one.

일체

몸과 마음은 일체
서로 따라 웃고 또 울지
같이 움츠리고 또 떨지

무수한 회로의 네트워크
헤아릴 수 없는 무선 신호
긴밀히 연결된 하나이지

쉴 새 없이 싸움하지만
끊을 수 없는 고리에 묶여
화해와 타협으로 정리되리

실로 이별하는 순간까지
다툼은 그침이 없지만
그래도 하나는 하나지

Threads

He devoted everything
To the land he cultivated and nurtured,
Surely, he could have protected it to the end.

But hunger and pain,
Worn down by loneliness,
Must have driven him away.

The last remaining chance
In this world-
He won't let it slip away.

The passion for duty
Was likely swept aside
By the pull of attachment.

Who knows how long it will last,
A soul weary from waiting-
Who will gather and sort right from wrong?

Is everything writhing in this world
But threads of a tapestry,
Wondrously being woven together?

실오라기

모두를 바쳐
그가 일구고 가꾼 땅
끝까지 지킬 법한데

허기와 고통
외로움에 지쳐
떠나갔으리

마지막 남은
이 세상 기회를
잃지 않겠단다

임무의 열정이
애착의 끌림에
밀려났으리

언제까지일지 몰라
기다림에 지친 영혼
잘잘못을 누가 갈무리하나

꿈틀대는 세상의 모두
놀랍게 짜여나갈
융단 실오라기들인지

Grace Period

Half-shed November trees,
Today the wind is resting,
Embraced by the tender sunlight,
A grace period has been granted-how long, I wonder.

Some fiery rebels cry out
That a reprieve is harsher than execution,
Yet most quietly wish for it deep inside,
Isn't all life, after all,
But a grace period in itself?

Not knowing when it will end,
We play games, sing songs, and dance away.
But on the day the time is set for execution,
The whole world within will tremble and sway.

유예기간

반쯤 벗겨진 11월 나무들
오늘따라 바람이 자고
따스한 빛살에 안겨 있지
얼마일지 유예기간을 맞았지

유예는 집행보다 가혹하다고
외치는 다혈질 반항아 있으나
대부분 내심으론 은근히 바라지
모든 삶은 본시 유예기간 아닌지

언제까지 일지 모르기에
게임하고 노래하며 춤추리
집행 시간이 잡히는 날엔
안 세상이 많이 요동치리

Vestigial Eyes

On a day when the earth's axis shakes,
In the dead of night as the ground collapses,
With the sky offering no response,
We lament and cast blame.

If we can't hear it, we say it doesn't exist,
Mistaking it for noise and passing it by.
If we can't see it, we say it doesn't exist,
Confusing it for something else and ignoring it.

Vestigial ears of you and me,
Trapped within the audible range.
Vestigial eyes of me and you,
Bound by the visible spectrum.

흔적 눈

지축이 흔들리는 날
땅이 꺼지는 한밤중
하늘이 무응답이니
한탄하며 원망하리

못 들으니 없다 하리
딴소리로 알고 지나치리
못 보니 없다 하리
딴 걸로 알고 무시하리

가청범위에 갇힌
너와 나의 흔적 귀
가시광선에 묶인
나와 너의 흔적 눈

Emanation

On the day a whirlwind blows away fallen leaves,
The dreary drizzle comes and goes,
Playing a seesaw game with the sunlight.

Beneath a towering tree in a forest of decay,
A crimson maple branch blooms surprisingly,
Radiant in its vibrant beauty.
Once smothered under the shadows
Of majestic trees, silently surviving,
Now it burns with life in its given moment,
Erupting its condensed vitality into vibrant color.

Who breathed in this elegant vitality?
The vivacious emanation of hues defying decay,
A sacred eruption of colors where fury has sublimated.

발산

회오리가 낙엽을 날리는 날
음산한 안개비는 오락가락
햇살과 시소게임을 벌이지

조락의 숲속 큰 나무 밑에
놀랍게 핀 빨강 단풍 가지
눈부시게 발랄한 아름다움
우람한 나무들의 등살에 깔려
그늘에 숨어 숨죽이며 살더니
주어진 때를 불태워 장식하리
농축된 생기를 색깔로 뿜는다

누가 불어넣은 우아한 생기이지
조락을 이긴 발랄한 빛깔의 발산
분노가 승화된 거룩한 색깔의 분출

Escape

In the ICU,
There is no distinction between day and night.

One keeps plummeting
Through a pitch-black sky.
As the speed of descent accelerates,
The fear of a deep abyss grows,
And one struggles desperately.

Suddenly, blinding wings appear,
Sweep down, grasping the hand.
The instant hands meet,
All anxiety and fear vanish,
And one is embraced by the wonder of freedom.

As a few faint words resonate in the air,
The entire brain transforms
Into a fiery launchpad,
And, clutching those wings, the soul escapes.
"You've done well. This is a new beginning!"

In the ICU,
Joy and sorrow are always locked in a seesaw game.

탈출

중환자실에는 따로
낮과 밤이 없지

캄캄한 하늘에서
추락을 거듭하지
낙하 속도가 빨라지니
깊은 구렁이 두려워
몹시 발버둥 치지

별안간 눈부셔 볼 수 없는
날개가 덮쳐 손을 잡아채지
손과 손이 닿는 순간 돌연
불안과 공포가 모두 사라지지
놀라운 자유의 품에 안기네

무언가 두어 마디 소리가
울려오는 순간 온 두뇌가
화염의 발사대로 변하며
날개를 잡고 넋이 탈출하지
"수고했어 다시 시작이야!"

중환자실에서는 늘
희비가 시소게임을 하지

Part II
The Wind Always Blows

제2부
바람은 언제나 분다

The Wind Always Blows

The wind always blows,
Shaking hearts and souls,
To remind them of promises.
The wind stirs time,
So that insight may emerge.

The wind blows everywhere,
It scatters fallen leaves,
In the burial ground where snowflakes drift,
Swelling spring branches
To bloom with flower buds.

The wind is a messenger of revelation,
A prophet and a judge,
Awakening the soul to mark its time.
The outer eyes may weep in lament,
While the inner eyes rejoice in rapture.

The wind blows, within and without.
Is there anything in this world
That comes to be without the wind?
Where does it come from, where does it go?
Is not the whole itself the wind?

바람은 언제나 분다

바람은 언제나 분다
마음과 심령을 흔들어
약속을 상기시켜 주려
바람은 시간을 섞지
통찰이 돌아나오도록

바람은 어디나 불지
눈발 날리는 장지에서
가랑잎을 뿌려대지
봄 가지를 부풀려
꽃눈을 피워내지

바람은 계시의 메신저
영혼을 깨워 때를 알리는
예언자이며 심판자이지
겉눈은 탄식하게 되리
속눈은 기뻐 환호하리

바람이 불지 안과 밖에
바람 없이 이루어지는 게
세상에 하나라도 있으랴
어디서 와 어디로 가는지
세상은 모두 바람 아닌지

Attraction

Before hearing,
Before seeing,
The heart swells
With great expectation.

Drawn to something,
I rush forward,
Rejoicing at the encounter.

The fake that seems real,
The real that seems fake–
Even prophets are confused.

The foolish discard the real as fake,
The unfortunate believe the fake as real.
Where do folly and misfortune arise?
Who grants wisdom and fortune?

끌림

듣기도 전에
보기도 전에
큰 기대에
가슴 부풀지

무언가에 끌려
마주 대할 기쁨에
달려 나가리

진짜 같은 가짜
가짜 같은 진짜
선지자도 헷갈리지

진짜를 가짜라 버린 우매
가짜를 진짜로 믿는 불행
우매와 불행은 어디서 오나
현명과 행운은 누가 주는지

Daydream

Past the brilliance and fervor,
The winter mountain graced by the first snow,
It's now time for a pause.

The clouds, astonishing in their ever-changing forms,
The sound of the river flowing endlessly,
The wind brushing past, scattering dust,
Before long, the mountain drifts into a daydream.

Unfolding great wings without hesitation,
It roams the wondrous world of imagination,
Embraced deeply by the joy of freedom,
A joy no one can take away.

Do not disrupt the daydream.
The originality that leads new beginnings-
It all springs forth from here.

백일몽

광휘와 열광을 지나서
첫눈까지 받은 겨울 산
이제 휴게에 들 차례지

놀랍게 수시 변모하는 구름
하염없이 흐르는 강물 소리
티끌을 날리며 스치는 바람
어느새 산은 백일몽에 잠기지

큰 날개를 펴고 거리낌 없이
경이로운 상상의 세계를 누비리
아무도 빼앗아 갈 수 없는
자유의 기쁨에 깊이 안기리

백일몽을 훼방하지 마라
시작을 선도하는 독창력
모두 여기서 솟아오르지

Insight

Does the unanswered waiting
Fade the promise into obscurity?

Stepping over winter shadows,
I run across a barren field
Where fallen leaves scatter in the wind.

Am I running away,
Or chasing something in the distance?

On the path braving the headwind,
A sudden sleet strikes my face,
Blinding my vision.

Passion and insight
Do not always walk hand in hand.

혜안

대답 없는 기다림에
기약이 희미해 지시나

겨울 그림자를
밟고 넘으며
낙엽 날리는 벌판을
가로질러 달리지

도망치는 건가
쫓아가는 거리

역풍을 안고 가는 길에
난데없는 진눈깨비
얼굴을 때리고
눈을 가려오지

열정과 혜안은 늘
같이 가지는 않으리

Prescription

Cold winds blow through the winter forest,
All have become bare trees alike-
Has the ideal of fairness been realized?

Each being is unique in its way;
Though the appearance may seem alike,
The feelings within surely differ.

Through diversity, equity, and inclusion,
We strive to make up for shortcomings,
Yet the anger of reverse discrimination cannot be ignored.

Poverty will always remain somewhere,
Resentment will exist everywhere.
Whose prescription will be the best solution?

처방

찬바람 불어치는 겨울 숲
모두 하나같이 나목이 되었지
공정의 이상은 실현된 건지

개체는 각양각색이니
겉모습은 비슷이 보여도
안의 느낌은 같지 않으리

다양과 공평과 포용으로
부족한 점 보완하려 하지만
역차별의 분노도 무시 못 하리

언제나 가난은 남아 있고
어디나 원망은 있으리니
누구의 처방이 최적일까

Despair

Striving to create a splendid work,
Pleading for just a little more light,
Yet like autumn leaves under heavy snow,
The hues of despair deepen.

Many are those who begin,
But few are those who achieve.
No matter whom or what one blames,
The sorrow of despair will deeply linger.

In this world, there are those
Who somehow manage to get by,
And others who, no matter what,
Simply cannot live that way.

There are those who have the means
To let go and walk away,
And those who have been pushed
To the very edge, with no way out.

낙망

멋진 작품 지어가도록
빛을 좀 더 애원하더니
폭설을 맞는 가을 잎들
낙망의 색깔이 짙어가지

시작하는 자는 많으나
이루는 이는 드물다지
누구 무엇에 탓을 해도
낙망의 한은 크게 맺히리

세상에는 그럭저럭
살 수 있는 자가 있고
아무리 해도 그렇게는
못 사는 이가 있으리

버리고 떠날 수 있는
여건의 사람이 있고
이미 땅끝까지 밀려
어쩔 수 없는 이가 있지

The Hidden Stream

Though it seems mighty,
Fragile are the thoughts.

Though it appears intact,
A heart withers within.
Though laughter abounds,
A soul feels sadness and fear.

We are all, in our way,
Trees in winter's slumber.
A faint, small voice
Calling out to someone.

Beneath the frozen river,
Flows a hidden stream.

숨어 흐르는 강물

우람해 보이지만
나약한 생각

멀쩡히 보여도
시들어 가는 심정
희희낙락해도
슬프고 두려운 심령

우리는 누구나
동면하는 나무들
누군가를 불러대는
수줍은 작은 목소리

얼어붙은 강 밑에
숨어 흐르는 강물

Wounds

By the riverside in late autumn,
Amid the dense mist
Of the reed field,

Hesitant beauty lingers,
Unable to part, circling endlessly.

They say there is no such thing as coincidence,
Yet, in an unexpected, fierce snowstorm,
Everything is buried without a trace.

From a place where graceful melodies once lingered,
A mournful tune now flows.

Is the stage of chaos and anguish
A punishment unknowingly invited,
Or the sequence of a preordained script?

Will it leave behind deep wounds
That cannot be healed or undone?

상처

만추의 강변
안개 자욱한
갈대꽃밭

머뭇대는 아름다움
차마 못 떠나 맴돌리

우연은 세상에 없다는데
난데없는 거센 눈보라에
자취도 없이 묻혀버리지

우아한 선율이 서린 곳에서
애통의 곡조가 흘러나오지

아비규환의 무대는 진정
모르게 자초한 징벌인지
정해진 각본의 순서인지

이전으로 돌아갈 수 없는
깊은 상처를 안겨줄 건가

Winter Riverside

On a bench by the winter riverside,
A middle-aged woman,
Pressing down a deep sky-blue hat,
Wrapped in a red scarf,
Gazes upward, searching the blue sky.

For what reason, drawn by what,
She has come here, no one knows.
Yet the sound of deep sighs often escapes her-
Surely, something elusive weighs on her mind.

Reed flowers ripple in the breeze,
While pigeons gather atop riverside trees,
Cuddled under the gentle sunlight,
They all gaze at the distant sky in unison.

겨울 강가

겨울 강가 벤치에 앉은
짙은 하늘색 모자 눌러쓴
빨간 목도리 중년 여인
창공을 우러러 더듬는다

무엇 하러 무엇에 끌려
여기 나왔는지 알 길 없으나
큰 한숨 소리 자주 들리니
무언가 안 잡히는 게 있으리

갈대꽃이 바람에 물결치는
강변 숲 나무 위 비둘기 무리
포근한 빛살 웅크려 쪼이며
하나같이 바라보는 먼 하늘

Drawing Lots

Is drawing lots
The most objective
And fair judgment
In the world?

Rolling a die,
Claiming the result
To be heaven's will–
How can that be proven?

Spinning a lottery machine,
To receive rewards or penalties,
To decide life or death–
Who guarantees its fairness?

Do we think this way,
Act this way,
And live believing
It is heaven's will?

제비뽑기

제비뽑기가
세상에서 가장
객관적이고
공정한 판정인지

주사위를 굴려
뽑히는 게
하늘의 뜻이지
입증은 쉽지 않으리

추첨기를 돌려
상과 벌을 받지
생사를 가르지
누가 보장한 공정인지

이렇게 생각하며
이렇게 행하며
하늘의 뜻이라고
믿고 살아가는지

A Striking Sensation

A thought suddenly pierces through-

Is it a glimmer amidst the light,
Or the beckoning temptation of darkness?

A fleeting, striking sensation-

Could it be the transcendent ecstasy of emotion,
Or the erupting ferocity of primal instincts?

A soul trembling to its roots-

Is it the awe of heaven's gates opening,
Or the horror of a hellish catastrophe?

강렬한 느낌

문득 파고드는 생각-

빛 가운데서 번득이는지
어둠이 손짓하는 유혹인지

스치는 강렬한 느낌-

감성의 초월적 황홀일지
분출하는 야수적 충동일지

뿌리가 떨리는 심령-

하늘 문이 열리는 경외인지
아비규환의 참상인지

Part III
The Drummer

제3부
북 치는 사람

The Drummer

Gathering all the strength within,
Immersed in ecstasy,
Solemnly and boldly,
The drummer strikes the drum.

When his turn has passed,
Until the next opportunity,
With a profound expression,
He waits for the right moment.

As the next movement begins,
The chance will return again.
The conductor will signal,
Following the composer's score.

Life is a series of waiting,
A rosary of returning chances,
An endless chain of encounters,
The drummer's devoted strikes.

Even when the performance ends,
It's not the end of everything.
Even when this world ends,
Not everything will come to an end.

북 치는 사람

온몸의 힘을 모아
황홀에 잠겨서
엄숙하게 담대히
북을 두드리지

차례가 지나니
다음 기회까지
심오한 표정으로
때를 기다리지

다음 악장이 열리며
기회는 다시 오리
지휘자가 눈짓하리
작곡자의 악보대로

세상은 기다림의 연속
다시 올 기회의 염주
끝없는 만남의 사슬
고수의 지극한 두드림

연주가 끝난다 해도
모두가 끝난 건 아니리
이 세상이 다 끝난다 해도
모두가 끝나는 건 아니리

An Immortal Glimpse

Drawn by something unknown,
They ascend to the base camp,
Gazing toward the summit
With steadfast and resolute eyes.

The mountains and fields glow in astonishing light,
The murmurs of streams flow through the valleys,
Autumn winds rustle the forest–
They are left speechless by the scenery.

Though water, wind, and colors
May flow and pass by,
The immortal glimpse and its resonance
Will seep deeply, etched forever within.

불후의 일별

무엇에 끌려서인지
베이스캠프에 올라
정상을 바라보는
의연한 그들의 눈빛

산야는 놀라운 빛에 물들고
계곡에 흐르는 냇물 소리
가을바람 타고 숲을 흔들지
그들은 풍광에 말을 잃었지

물과 바람과 빛깔은
흘러가고 스쳐 가도
불후의 일별과 울림은
깊이 배어들어 새겨지리

A Cozy Night

A cozy night,
A snug slumber,
Do you plead for
Dreams sweet and serene?

In a mundane, tedious world,
Will it not suffocate?
Without a kaleidoscope of hues,
How can masterpieces be painted?

Though it may seem different on the surface,
In truth, it's all the same.
Even within a cozy, sweet dream,
A stage of endless change unfolds.

Whatever may transpire,
Whatever the outcome may be,
A profound meaning lies within-
The dream you sought is already fulfilled.

포근한 밤

포근한 밤
아늑한 잠
단꿈을 꾸게
간구하느냐

단조하고 지루한 세상
숨 막히지 않을 건지
변화무쌍한 색채 없이
걸작이 어찌 그려지리

겉으로는 달리 보여도
실은 다를 바 없으리
포근한 단꿈 안에도
변화무쌍한 무대가 있지

어떤 상황이 벌어지고
무슨 결과를 맺어도
깊은 뜻이 담겨 있으리니
간구의 꿈을 이미 이루었지

Nostalgia

At the sight of the setting sea,
Nostalgia stirs suddenly,
Would you dismiss it as a trite trinket,
Casting it aside with a scornful remark?

The farther and deeper you venture,
You shall meet solitude and despair.
You might long to hear the breath of origin,
And feel the rhythm of your true heartbeat.
Isn't nostalgia a longing
Deeply rooted in the soul, unshakable?

Nostalgia serves as a moment to turn back,
Rearranging the order of things.
Earthly nostalgia fades with time,
As the longing for the heavens begins to grow.

향수

저무는 바다 풍경에
문득 향수가 꿈틀대지
진부한 노리개라고
일갈에 내치려는가

멀리 깊이 들어갈수록
외로움과 낭패와 마주하리
태초의 숨소리 듣고 싶으리
본래의 심장박동이 느껴지리
향수는 영혼 깊이 박힌
떨칠 수 없는 동경 아닌지

향수는 돌이키는 계기
순서를 재정비케 하리
땅의 향수는 빛이 바래가며
하늘의 향수가 자라오르지

The Elevator

One day, we shall step into the elevator,
And journey across the depths of the cosmos.
Beyond the times of gazing and meditation,
We hope to be embraced by profound comfort.

Crowds clashing in a battle to rise,
Blind masses locked in fierce competition,
Clowns climbing ropes, their souls adrift,
Beasts wandering the earth to sate their hunger.
The elevator's arrival signal
Flashes as it draws ever nearer.

When dignity triumphs over arrogance,
When principles dispel attachment-
Who will be the first to step aboard?
What will resist until the very end?

승강기

언젠가는 승강기에 올라
심우주를 누비게 되리
응시와 명상의 시간 너머
큰 위로에 안기길 바라지

오르려 대결하는 무리
눈멀어 각축하는 인파
혼 잃고 밧줄 타는 광대
채우려 땅을 헤매는 짐승
승강기의 도착 신호가
번득이며 다가오고 있지

존엄이 자만을 이길 때리
법도가 애착을 물릴 때리
누가 맨 처음 타게 되는지
무엇이 끝까지 거스를 건지

The Fox and the Bear

The battle between the fox and the bear
Reaches its climactic stage.
The cunning fox ensnares the witless bear,
Trapping it in a clever scheme.
The referee, swayed by the louder cheer,
Is too busy reading the room.

What do the eyes of the world
Use to glimpse the future?
Eyes that wait for stars
In the night sky
Will look to the stump
For sprouts to bloom.

In the realm of foxes and bears,
Beyond envy, greed, and distrust,
What else can be seen or hoped for?
Is there insight to discern the truth,
The courage to make it real,
And a cosmic aspiration embedded within?

여우와 곰

여우와 곰의 싸움이
진입 가경에 접어들지
간사한 여우 꼬임에 걸려
재치 없는 곰이 함정에 빠지지
주심은 어느 응원 소리가 큰지
눈치 보기에 여념이 없다

세상눈은 무엇으로
미래를 가늠하는지
밤하늘에서 별을
기다리는 눈은
그루터기서 피어날
새싹을 바라보리

여우나 곰의 나라에서
시기와 탐욕과 불신 외에
무엇이 보이고 기대되는지
간파할 통찰력이 있는지
실현할 용기가 있는지
우주적 염원이 담겼는지

Illiteracy and Ignorance

The world is said to be
An arena where reason and emotion collide.

Politicians ignorant of science
Try to rule over reason,
While scientists unaware of politics
Attempt to instruct emotion.

Civilization is a revolving stage
Where illiteracy and ignorance brawl.
Will emotion subjugate reason,
Or will reason dominate emotion?

The victor crowned with the champion's belt-
What does it seek to proclaim?
The whisper of the fallen loser-
What does it hold within?

We know what is missing,
But we can't see where it belongs.

문맹과 무지

세상은 이성과 감성이
격돌하는 경기장이라지

과학 문맹의 정치가
이성을 다스리려 하지
정치 무지의 과학이
감성을 가르치려 하지

문명은 문맹과 무지가
난투하는 회전무대
감성이 이성을 석권하려나
이성이 감성을 압도하려나

챔피언 띠를 두른 승자
무엇을 선포하려는지
쓰러지는 패자의 귓속말
그 안에 무엇이 들어 있나

무엇이 **빠져** 있는지는 알지만
그게 들어설 자리는 안 보이네

Disposal

The world is an endless assembly line
Of creation and disposal.
A marvelous journey,
From eternity and back to eternity.

Who is exempt from being disposed of?
When the fleeting fanfare fades,
They follow the line in due course.
As the speed of civilization's advances grows,
The process of disposal accelerates in turn.

Traces of victory and defeat,
Imprints of joy and anguish,
All are burned away, leaving only the essence,
To become the next stage's new creation.

처분

세상은 생성과 처분의
끝없는 일관작업 라인
영원에서 와 영원으로
돌아가는 놀라운 여정

처분의 대상 아닌 자 누군가
한때의 팡파르가 스쳐 가면
순서를 따라 그 길로 들어서지
문명의 이기 속도에 비례하여
처분의 과정도 가속화되어 가리

승리와 패배의 흔적
환희와 고뇌의 심상
말끔히 태워 버리고 진수만
다음 단계의 신제품이 되지

Consideration

Who are you waiting for?
What are you trying to grasp?
You run forward, believing you'll meet,
You chase ahead, convinced you'll catch.

Endless waiting with no guarantee-
A hidden promise unseen.
Uncertain hopes without assurance-
The eyes of consideration that see beyond.

Worries, sorrows, pain, and grief-
Gentle feelers placed to prevent falling,
Delicate and compassionate in their design-
Truly, a marvelous creation.

배려

누구를 기다리는지
무엇을 잡아보려나
만날 거라고 달려가지
잡게 되리라 쫓아가리

기약 없는 기다림은
안 보이게 넣어준 약속
보장 없는 기대는
너머를 볼 배려의 눈

걱정 근심도 슬픔과 아픔도
넘어져 다치지 않게 넣어준
세심하고 자비로운 더듬이들
실로 경이로운 디자인이지

The Final Gaze
- In Memory of Sister Nansoon

On an early day in the bitter December winds,
When fallen leaves scatter in the chill,
The heartbreaking news crosses the sea-
From Yangpyeong to Seoul, from Laos to Iran,
From Virginia to New York, her tumultuous journey
Reaches its end in a solitary room, far from home.

They say her mind stayed sharp until the very end,
Yet her final path must have been steep and rugged.
Her nightly cries for help still echo in memory,
Battling the terrifying shadows of darkness.
That final glance exchanged with her younger sister,
A gaze filled with indescribable love, sorrow, and plea-

Life comes and goes, aligned with the laws of nature.
As a beloved first daughter, she grew up cherished,
Smiling and crying, witnessing an era of chaos.
Her fearful struggle to hold on to life has now ended.
In the eternal land where death exists no more,
She rests, cradled in the warm embrace of freedom and peace.

마지막 시선
- 난순 누나를 애도하며

찬바람에 낙엽이 날리는 섣달 초
요양원에서 사투하던 난순 누나
떨리는 비보가 바다를 건너 든다
양평서 서울로 라오스서 이란으로
버지니아서 뉴욕으로 파란만장의
여정이 이역만리 독방서 막 내리지

끝까지 정신이 흐리지 않았다니
마지막 가는 길이 험난했으리
밤마다 도움을 간청하던 외침
무서운 어둠의 그림자와의 싸움
여동생과 마주했던 마지막 시선
형용할 수 없는 애착 비애 애원-

섭리에 맞춰 오고 돌아가는 길
귀염둥이 첫딸로 사랑으로 자라
웃고 울며 혼돈의 시대를 마감했지
숨을 지키려던 두려운 씨름은 끝나고
더는 죽음이 없는 영원의 나라에서
자유와 평화의 큰 품에 포근히 안기지

Doubt and Worry

Do the clouds arrive
As prayed for?
Does the wind fulfill
What is believed?

Whether things will turn out as thought-
That, we'll only know by stepping in.
We worry, so we pray;
We doubt, yet deep inside, we believe.

Worry is the source of prayer,
Doubt the beginning of faith.
A door that cannot be opened alone,
A handle grasped only with help.

의심과 걱정

간구대로 구름은
도달하게 되는 건가
믿는 대로 바람은
이루게 되는 걸까

여기 생각대로 될지는
들어가 보아야 알겠으니
걱정되니 기원하리
의심하며 안으론 믿으리

근심은 기도의 원천
의심은 믿음의 시작
혼자서는 열 수 없는 문
도와줘야 잡히는 문고리

Part IV
Smile

제4부
미소

The Wheel

Time is an incredible wheel
That rolls on without end.
Countless tiny bubbles rise,
Only to burst and vanish again.

Victors of the moment, losers to time,
Living within time, departing in an instant.
Are we merely dragged along,
Or do we also steer it, somehow?

The moment you truly wished
Time would stop-
When was it for you?
Where was it for me?

Whose time is it now?
What moment are we living?
Is it a game of deception,
A stage of killing and being killed?

Whose time comes next?
What will that time be for?
A contest of understanding and awakening,
A world of saving and truly living.

바퀴

시간은 그침 없이
굴러가는 놀라운 바퀴
무수한 작은 거품이
왜인지 일고 또 꺼져가지

순간의 승자요 시간의 패자
시간에 살다 순간에 가지
오로지 끌려만 가는 건가
실로 이끌기도 하는 건지

흘러가지 않길
진정 바라던 순간이
너에겐 언제이지
나에겐 어디이지

지금은 누구의 때
무얼 하는 순간이지
속고 속이는 경기이지
죽이고 죽는 무대이지

다음은 누구의 때
무얼 할 시간인지
깨닫고 깨우는 시합이리
살리고 사는 세상이리

Sprouting Shoots

The greater the expectation,
The greater the disappointment in proportion.
So I resolve to expect no more,
Arm with determination as I step out,
Only to return once again, burdened with disappointment.

They say missed opportunities
Never come back again.
Yet on the shimmering horizon,
What is it I still hope for?
Where does the hope rise anew
That it might return in a different guise?

No matter how much I suppress and cover,
How can I stop the sprouting shoots?
Disappointment, in truth, is the launchpad of longing.
Though now a frozen wasteland,
Soon a green tide will sweep across the earth.

돋아나는 싹

기대가 크면 그만큼
실망도 비례하리니
더는 기대하지 말자고
완전 무장하고 나가선
또 실망을 안고 돌아오리

지나간 기회는 다시
돌아오지 않는다는데
어른거리는 지평에서
무엇을 기대하는지
다른 옷 입고 다가오리란
희망은 어디서 솟아나는지

아무리 짓눌러 덮으려 해도
돋아나는 싹을 어찌 막으랴
실망은 실로 갈망의 발사대
지금은 얼어붙은 동토이지만
초록 물결이 곧 천지를 덮으리

Judgment Day

Maximizing sensuality,
They say it summons elegance.
Exposing the full extent of demonic allure,
They claim it spreads divinity.

Will you build a kingdom of righteousness
By making wickedness your vanguard?

Praying through tear-filled nights,
Asking to resemble the ultimate good.
In a dreamlike trance,
You saw a vision-
You stood there with Him.

The outward appearance bore similarity,
Yet within lurked a writhing demon.

Venturing into the wilderness, day and night,
Realizing the love of devotion.
Even after washing and cleansing
The inherent nature of evil,
Is Judgment Day still inevitable?

It is a day of triumph,
Eradicating the hidden germs within the sick,
Bringing forth the dawn of complete healing.

심판의 날

관능을 극대화하여
우아를 불러드린단다
마성을 최대로 노출해
신성을 전파하련다네

사악을 선봉장으로 세워
의의 나라를 세우려느냐

지고선을 닮게 해달라
눈물로 지새워 기도하더니
비몽사몽간에 환상을 보네
그와 함께 선 저를 보았지

겉모습은 비슷이 닮았는데
속에 숨어 꿈틀대는 마수

광야에 밤낮으로 나아가
헌신의 사랑을 깨닫고
마의 근성을 씻고 씻겨도
심판의 날은 불가피한 건가

환자의 숨은 병독을 섬멸해
완치시키는 개선의 날이지

Spacefaring

Amid the rays of the setting sun,
The treetops stand tall and high.
Immersed in the joy of anticipation,
Unable to hide their revealing smiles.

Under the deepening night sky,
Preparing to greet the meteor shower.
Riding the cascading streams of light,
They embark on a journey through space.

Circling the outskirts of the solar system,
Gliding past interstellar landscapes,
Reaching the peak of the Milky Way,
Reveling in the sight of the universe's expansion.

Do not mistake it for a desolate wasteland.
It is a stage pulsating with the heat of life,
Where thoughts and emotions dance,
Carrying the profound message of the soul.

Ceaselessly calling,
Irresistibly drawing us in.
With the archetype deeply ingrained,
The signal of its call is unmistakable.

우주여행

석양의 빛살 가운데
높이 머리든 우듬지
기다리는 큰 기쁨에 잠겨
드러나는 미소를 못 감추지

깊어 가는 밤하늘에서
유성우 맞을 채비를 하지
쏟아지는 빛줄기를 타고
우주여행에 오를 심산이지

태양계의 외곽을 둘러
성 간 풍물을 스쳐 지나
은하수 꼭대기에 이르지
우주 팽창 모습을 만끽하리

삭막한 황야로 오해 마시게
모든 생각과 느낌이 춤추는
영혼의 메시지가 깊이 담긴
뜨거운 생명의 박동 무대이지

끊임없이 부르기에
한없이 끌려가지
원형이 깊이 내재하기에
부르는 신호를 감지하리

The Root of Supplication

The mysterious path of return,
An unfathomable truth
Beyond the realm of our ability-
How is it that the unknown
Can make us tremble so with fear?

Just as curiosity serves as a tool for discovery,
Surely fear and sorrow, too,
Are the deep roots of earnest supplication,
Yearning to be held in merciful arms,
To find freedom and peace.

As all organs and systems
Are interconnected with the brain's core,
So too are thoughts and feelings of fear
Tightly intertwined,
Both wired and wireless, with the source of life.

Unavoidable thoughts,
Feelings that surge within,
And a reverent spirit-
All are bound together
In an unbreakable chain,
Forged deeply at the dawn of creation.

간구의 뿌리

되돌아가는 오묘한 길
진상을 파악할 수 없는
능력 밖 영역인데
모르는 게 어찌 이처럼
두려워 떨게 하는지

호기심이 추구의 도구이듯
두려움과 슬픔은 분명
자비로운 큰 팔에 안겨
자유와 평화를 누리고 싶은
지극한 간구의 뿌리이지

모든 장기와 시스템이
뇌 중추와 고리 지어 있듯
두려움의 생각과 느낌이
생명의 원천에 긴밀하게
유선 무선으로 엮여 있지

피할 수 없는 생각
밀려 들어오는 느낌
경외하는 심령 모두
태초에 깊이 결속된
끊을 수 없는 고리지

How Fragile We Are

Will you become a tool of jealousy?
Will you fall as a slave to anger?
Will you bow your knees to the devil?
For whom,
For what purpose,
Would you do such things?

Opening the best path before you,
Watching over you day and night with devotion,
Teaching and refining the way
To vanquish evil-
Yet, mercilessly crushed
By the wicked spirits of greed, distrust, and rebellion.

How terrifying,
The emotions of humanity.
How foolish,
The intellect of humanity.
How fragile,
The spirituality of humanity.

얼마나 허약한지

시기의 도구가 되려느냐
분노의 노예로 전락하려나
마귀에게 무릎 꿇으려나
누구 때문에
무엇을 위해
이런 짓을 하려나

가장 좋은 길을 열어주고
열의로 밤낮 지켜주며
마성을 섬멸하는 길을
가르치고 연마시키지만
탐욕과 불신과 반역의
악령에 무참히 짓밟히지

얼마나 무서운지
인간의 감성
얼마나 어리석은지
인간의 지성
얼마나 허약한지
인간의 영성

Joy and Comfort

Even in the polar chill of the Arctic
And the icy seas of the Antarctic,
Though clumsy in their own way,
Joy and comfort will surely abide.

The joy of feeding and being fed,
The mercy of clothing and being clothed,
The comfort of enjoying and sharing–
These will always dwell with life.

Through rotation and revolution,
Joy and comfort rain down,
Equally shining on all,
Yet received only as much as opened to.

Joy and comfort are
Fair and abundant,
But whether welcomed or refused,
They overflow or run dry.

기쁨과 위로

북극의 한파 속에나
남극의 얼음 바다에도
어설프나 나름대로
기쁨과 위로는 있으리

먹이고 먹는 기쁨
입고 입히는 자비
누리고 누려주는 위로
언제나 삶과 함께하리

자전과 공전으로
내려주는 기쁨과 위로
똑같이 쪼여주지만
여는 만큼만 받게 되리

기쁨과 위로는
공평하고 풍성한데
환영인지 거절인가로
넘치고 메마르리

The Face of the Winter Solstice

Trapped in a tunnel of darkness
That seems to have no end,
Shall I fall into the panic of illusion?

The face of the winter solstice
Is painted in the winter sky.
Within the swirling clouds,
Rays of light seep through, opening
A breathtaking, vast, and deep expanse–
A space filled with infinite possibilities.

Riding on the dazzling starlight of the night sky,
The sun hastens its return,
Shaking the earth's axis with majestic footsteps.

동지의 얼굴

끝이 없을 것 같은
어둠의 터널에 갇혀
착시의 공황에 빠지려나

동짓날의 얼굴은
겨울 하늘에 그려 있지
구름의 소용돌이 안으로
빛살이 스미며 열리는
놀라운 높고 깊은 창공
무한 가능성이 담겨 있지

눈부신 밤하늘 별빛 타고
바삐 달려 돌아오는 태양
웅장한 발소리로 지축을 흔들지

Mother's Eyes

On the southern seaside,
A dazzling sandy beach surprises,
A two-year-old grabs a handful of sand
And asks her mom,

"Is all of this snow?"
Her innocent, sparkling eyes
Reflect the smile of the sky.
She toddles toward the sea,
Dipping her feet into the water.

"Soon enough,
She'll demand the sea, the sandy beach,
And even the blue sky to be hers!"
The mother's eyes gaze at her softly,
Lost in thought.

엄마 눈

남쪽 나라 바닷가
눈부신 모래밭에 놀라
모래 한 줌 움켜쥐고
엄마한테 묻는 두 살짜리 딸

"이게 다 눈이야!?"
순진만 담긴 초롱 눈
하늘의 미소가 흐르지
아장아장 바닷물로
발을 잠가 들어가지

"얼마 있으면 곧
바다 모래밭 푸른 하늘
모두 사달라 떼쓰리!"
물끄러미 바라보는 엄마 눈

The Square Jungle

No matter what schemes are devised,
No matter what weapons are wielded,
You must strike the opponent to the ground.

As foolish as they are, as wise as they are,
They will throw punches.
As learned as they are, as ignorant as they are,
They will lash out with kicks.

As the fight drags on,
The reason for fighting is forgotten,
And winning becomes the sole purpose.

Even in the square jungle,
Where not even the referee can intervene,
The voice of conscience,
Placed within them by someone,
Will be heard.

Whether victor or defeated,
When they return home and find themselves alone,
They'll turn their backs and quietly weep.

사각의 정글

무슨 계략을 쓰더라도
어떤 무기를 휘둘러서도
바닥에 때려눕혀야 하리

우매한 그대로 현명한 그대로
주먹질하리
유식한 그대로 무식한 그대로
발길질하리

한참 싸우다 보면
싸우는 이유도 모르고
이기는 게 목적이 되리

사각의 정글에도
주심도 어쩔 수 없는
누군가 그들 안에 넣어준
양심의 소리 들려오리

승자거나 패자거나
집에 돌아가 홀로 되면
등 돌리고 흐느끼리

Smile

The stern face of a grandmother
Bursts into a radiant smile
At the innocent smile of her grandson.

What did she see?
What moved her so deeply
That she couldn't contain her joy?

Does she catch a glimpse of the source of that smile?
Does the meaning of life flash before her?
Her grandson becomes her teacher.

The grandson, too young to recall this smile,
Will one day become a grandfather,
Awed by the smile of his granddaughter.

The astonishing exchange of smiles,
The mysterious awakening of smiles,
The marvel of smiles passed down through generations.

미소

근엄한 할머니 얼굴이
천진난만한 손자의
미소에 파안대소하지

무엇을 보았길래
무슨 감동이 일어나
기쁨을 주체 못 하는지

미소의 원천을 흘깃 보는지
삶의 의미가 스쳐 지나는지
손자가 할머니 선생이네

미소의 기억도 없는 손자
먼 훗날 할아버지가 되어
손녀의 미소에 감복하리

놀라운 미소의 교환
오묘한 미소의 환기
경탄할 미소의 유전

Part V
Order

제5부
질서

Reemergence

As the gates of heaven open,
The deeply instilled emotions
Stir the mind and heart,
Reemerging the symphony of the essence.

Do you see that breathtaking scenery?
It is drawn just as reflected on the face.
The melody reveals the heavens above,
The song unveils the pinnacle of the sublime.

As written in the score,
Gazes and movements of hands unite,
Shaking the heart and soul,
Recreating the glory of the original.

Resonating through the universe,
The reenactment of awe,
Racing toward eternity,
A chain of endless reemergence.

재현

하늘 문이 열리며
깊이 부어 넣어준 감동
머리와 가슴을 격동해
본체의 연주를 재현하리

저 황홀한 경관 보이지
얼굴에 그려진 대로지
선율이 드러내는 하늘나라
노래가 펼치는 숭고의 극치

악보에 그려진 대로
눈빛과 손놀림이 모여
마음과 심령을 흔들어서
본디의 영광을 재현하지

우주로 울려 퍼지는
감동의 재현
영원으로 달려가는
재현의 사슬고리

Paradox

There must be someone who pretends to be deceived when you try to deceive.

There must be someone who pretends to lose when you try to win.

There must be someone who pretends to die when you wish to kill.

There is nothing that is not a revelation.
Have you ever seen anything that is not a miracle?
The miracle of paradox,
The revelation of paradox,
The world of paradox.

The place of defeat becomes the seat of victory.
The day of sorrow will be greeted by joy.
The fear of death turns into the rapture of life.

역설

속이려고 할 때 속은 척해 준 이 있으리
이기려 하기에 진 척해 준 이 있으리
죽이고 싶어 하니 죽은 척해 준 이 있으리

계시가 아닌 건
어디에도 없으리
기적이 아닌 것
본 적이 있는지
역설의 기적
역설의 계시
역설의 세상

패망의 장소가 승리의 자리지
슬픔의 날을 기쁨이 맞으리
죽음의 두려움이 삶의 환희가 되지

Waste

Do you lament and regret
The futile consumption of time and resources,
The waste of heart and soul?

Fruitless devotion and sacrifice,
Empty persuasion and reform,
A world that repays good with evil.

Where is the focus
Of your expectations and disappointments?
By what standard is it called waste?

What are you trying to illuminate?
The glory of heaven,
Or selfish ambition?

Every act that truly reveals
The glory of heaven alone
Will shine eternally with everlasting light.

낭비

헛된 시간과 재원의 소모
마음과 심령의 낭비라고
개탄하며 후회하시는지

결실 없는 헌신과 희생
헛도는 설득과 교화
선을 악으로 갚는 세상

어디에 초점을 맞춘
기대와 실망인지
무엇에 준거한 낭비인지

무엇을 조명하려느냐
하늘의 영광인지
이기적 야망인지

하늘의 영광만을 진정
드러내는 모든 행위
영원한 빛과 함께하리

Feed

In the snowy December chill,
Pigeons gather in flocks,
Hovering and glancing nervously,
Waiting for something to appear.

Even after waiting for a while,
Nothing comes their way.
With eyes full of disappointment,
They scatter off somewhere else.

"Even misers drop a crumb now and then,
But luck had it we got nothing today!"
Their faint trace of discontent seems to echo.

Embarrassed on the way back,
At the park entrance stands a sign:
"Do not feed the pigeons!"

모이

눈 내리는 섣달
모이 찾는 비둘기들
우르르 모여들어
서성대며 눈치만 보네

한참 기다려 보아도
무소식이니
실망의 눈빛 던지며
어딘가로 물러가지

"수전노도 가끔은 흘리는데
재수 없이 맹탕이 걸렸지!"
그들의 서운한 여운이 들려오리

무안해서 돌아오는 길
공원 입구의 주의 사항 가로되
"비둘기에 모이 주지 마세요!"

The Bond

In fury at rejection,
You cry out to sever ties,
Yet you can never break them.

At unrepentant wrongdoing,
You shout to cast them away,
Yet you can never abandon them.

Neither rebellion,
Nor punishment,
Can sever the bond.

For it was made this way,
Designed to be,
An unbreakable bond.

끈

거절에 크게 분노해
단절하리라 울부짖으나
결코 끊을 수 없으리

뉘우침 없는 악행에
내치리라 불호령하나
결코 내치지 못하리

반역도 하나
처벌도 하나
관계는 못 끊으리

그렇게 되도록
그렇게 디자인된
끊을 수 없는 끈

A Hint

Grasping only the edge,
Endlessly, the end appears.
Focusing solely on the end,
You'll only cling to its edge.

In the radiant bloom of flowers,
Do you not see the waving gestures within?
Amid the stars shining in the night sky,
Do you not hear the subtle whispers of a hint?

Grasping only the beginning,
You will see nothing but beginnings.
Fixating solely on the start,
There will be endless beginnings.

귀띔

끝자락만 잡으니
한없이 끝만 보이리
끝만 바라보기에
끝자락만 붙들게 되리

눈부시게 피어나는 꽃 무리
그 안에서 흔드는 손짓 보이지
밤하늘에 빛나는 별 무리
속삭이는 은밀한 귀띔 들리지

시작만 움켜쥐니
한없이 시작만 보이리
시작만 바라보기에
무한한 시작뿐이리

A Mark

Behold the lofty heavens above,
For the answer lies within.

A promise is inscribed there,
A mark deeply hidden away,
The path to follow is drawn within.

Who dares to call it void?
Wandering, for they see no sign.

For their hearts are clouded,
For their spirits are hollow,
They cannot grasp the mark.

Lift your eyes and gaze deeply,
The radiant heavens await with the mark.

징표

바라보아라 드높은 창공
바로 그 안에 답이 있지

거기에 약속이 쓰여 있지
징표를 깊이 숨겨두었지
가야 할 길이 그려져 있지

누가 공허뿐이라느냐
징표를 못 보니 헤매리

흐려진 마음이기에
공허한 심령이기에
징표를 못 붙들리

눈을 들어 깊이 바라보라
징표가 기다리는 눈부신 창공

Witch Hunt

Are all ingenious ideas
Inspired from above?
The outburst of selfish ambition,
Or the hidden demon's convulsion?

Countless extraordinary thoughts
Dig their own graves.

In the piercing gaze of witch hunters,
The devil's schemes flicker.
Gun barrels aiming for bounties—
Who is the criminal, and who the enforcer?

The path to building a heaven on earth
Turns into an unrelenting spree of slaughter.

The cunning revelation
Of a false prophet
Offers children as sacrifices
To the devil's altar.

A democratic state, trembling before the might of fandoms,
Pitifully tucking its tail in submission.

마녀사냥

기발한 아이디어가 모두
위에서 내린 영감인지
이기적 야심의 발산일지
숨어 있는 악마의 발작인지

수많은 비상한 생각이
자신의 무덤을 파가지

마녀 사냥꾼의 눈초리에
마귀의 책략이 번듯거리지
현상금 노리는 총부리들
누가 범죄자이고 집행자인지

지상천국을 세우는 길이
무자비 학살의 자행이네

거짓 선지자의
기발한 계시가
악마의 제물로
자녀를 바치지

팬덤의 위세에 벌벌 떨며
가련히 꼬리 내린 민주국가

Archaeologist

The gaze of an archaeologist,
The glare of a clown.

Their focus is worlds apart,
Yet their purpose, not so far.
They look down on each other,
Yet envy one another as well.

Which do you admire?
Which do you despise?

Whether you admit it or not,
Both are reflections of everyone's self.
Not a difference in kind, but in degree,
Their phenotype is revealed.

고고학자

고고학자의 눈빛
어릿광대의 눈초리

초점은 생판 다르지만
목적은 유사하지
서로 업신여기지만
서로 부러워도 하리

어느 걸 선망하시지
어느 걸 혐오하시지

인정하든 않든 둘 다
누구나의 자화상이지
질이 아닌 양의 차이로
표현형이 드러나지

Counterattack

Nowhere left to run,
Pushed to the edge of a cliff.
There's no choice but to face it,
Charging forward,
Fear vanishes.

The readiness to counter,
The strength to fight-
Though it seems absent within me,
Where does it arise?
Surely, someone stands with me.

Carried by the greatest strength,
It will overcome all else.
Lifted to the highest pedestal,
None can follow its lead.
The flag of victory will be waved high.

응전

더는 도망칠 데 없어
낭떠러지에 밀리니
맞설 수밖에 없으리
달려 들어가니
무서움이 사라지네

응전할 태세
싸울 힘
제 안에 없을 듯한데
어디서 솟아오르지
분명 누군가 함께하리

가장 큰 힘에 업히니
다른 모든 걸 이기리
가장 높이 추켜들어 주니
아무도 따라올 수 없으리
승리의 깃발을 나부껴 주리

Order

The ultrasound reveals
The maturing form of a fetus,
A miracle sprouting wondrously
From a single fertilized cell.

The power bestowed at creation,
A life code of planning and execution,
Astonishing order embedded in genes,
Unfolding the rhythm of time's design.
The head follows its designated path-
The heart and lungs develop as they're led-
Every system, as determined,
Grows and differentiates with perfect order.

Through the power of awe-inspiring order,
The present, encoded in the past,
The future, encrypted in the present,
Blooms into marvelous forms.

질서

초음파 영상에 잡힌
성숙해 가는 태아 모습
수태된 한 세포로부터
놀랍게 돋아나는 기적

태초에 내려받은 권능
계획과 실행의 생명 코드
유전자에 담긴 경탄할
시간의 질서가 발휘되지
지정된 길 따라 머리가-
 이끌어 가는 대로 심폐가-
결정된 대로 모든 시스템이-
질서 정연히 분화 성장하지

경외한 질서의 능력으로
과거 안에 코드로 담긴 현재가
현재 안에 암호로 안긴 미래가
경이로운 형상들로 피어 나가지

| Epilogue |

Silent Knocks

How many knocks
Turn into silent ones,
Passing by without an answer?

Always knocking at the door,
But no one listens carefully,
Unable to hear,
Believing no one is there.

The silent knock
Waits endlessly
For ears that can hear.

| 에필로그 |

소리 없는 노크

얼마나 많은 두드림이
소리 없는 노크가 되어
대답 없이 스쳐 가는지

언제나 문 앞에서
두드리는데
기울여 듣지 않으니
못 듣고 없는 줄로 알지

소리 없는 노크
들을 수 있는 귀를
한없이 기다리리

About the Author
Lee Won-Ro

Poet as well as medical doctor (cardiologist), professor, chancellor of hospitals and university president, Lee Won-Ro's career has been prominent in his brilliant literary activities along with his extensive experiences and contributions in medical science and practice.

Lee Won-Ro is the author of sixty one poetry books along with fourteen anthologies. He also published extensively including ten books related to medicine both for professionals and general readership.

Lee Won-Ro's poetic world pursues the fundamental themes with profound aesthetic enthusiasm. His work combines wisdom and knowledge derived from his scientific background with his artistic power stemming from creative imagination and astute intuition.

Lee Won-Ro's verse embroiders refined tints and serene tones on the fabric of embellished words.

Poet Lee Won-Ro explores the universe in conjunction with his expertise in intellectual, affective and spiritual domains as a specialist in medicine and science to create his unique artistic world.

This book along with "Five Seasons", "The Sower", "Vertical and Horizontal", "That Day, That Moment", "The Sound of Waves", "Weather Vane", "Countdown", "On the Road", "Winter Gift", "Fair Winds", "Spiral Staircase", "The Watershed", "The Seed of Eternity", "Milky Way In DNA", "Signs of Recovery", "Applause", "Invitation", "Night Sky", "Revival", "The Promise", "Time Capsule", "The Tea Cup and the Sea", "The Tunnel of Waves", "The Tomorrow within Today", "Flowers and Stars", "Corona Panic", "Chorus", "Waves", "Thanks and Empathy", "Red Berries", "Dialogue", "A Mural of Sounds", "Focal Point", "Day Break", "Prelude to a Pilgrimage", "Rehearsal", "TimeLapse Panorama", "Eve Celebration", "A Trumpet Call", "Right on Cue", "Why Do You Push My Back", "Space Walk", "Phoenix Parade", "The Vortex of Dances", "Pearling", "Priming Water", "A Glint of Light", "The River Unstoppable", "Song of Stars", "The Land of Floral Buds", "A Flute Player", "The Glow of a Firefly", "Resonance", "Wrinkles in Time", "Wedding Day", "Synapse". "Miracles are Everywhere", "Unity in Variety" and "Signal Hunter" are available at Amazon.com/author/leewonro or kdp.amazon.com/book shelf(paperbacks and e-books).

글쓴이
이원로

　시인이자 의사(심장전문의), 교수, 명예의료원장, 전 대학교총장인 이원로 시인은 월간문학으로 등단, 이번 시집과 더불어 "빛과 소리를 넘어서", "햇빛 유난한 날에", "청진기와 망원경", "팬터마임", "피아니시모", "모자이크", "순간의 창", "바람의 지도", "우주의 배꼽", "시집가는 날", "시냅스", "기적은 어디에나", "화이부동", "신호추적자", "시간의 주름", "울림", "반딧불", "피리 부는 사람", "꽃눈 나라", "별들의 노래", "멈출 수 없는 강물", "섬광", "마중물", "진주 잡이", "춤의 소용돌이", "우주유영", "어찌 등을 미시나요", "불사조 행렬", "마침 좋은 때에", "나팔소리", "전야제", "타임랩스 파노라마", "장도의 서막", "새벽", "초점", "소리 벽화" "물결", "감사와 공감", "합창", "코로나 공황", "대화", "뻘간 열매", "꽃과 별", "바람 소리", "우리집", "오늘 안의 내일", "파도의 터널", "찻잔과 바다", "타임 캡슐", "약속", "소생", "밤하늘", "초대장", "박수갈채", "회복의 눈빛", "DNA 안 은하수", "영원의 씨", "분수령", "나선 계단", "순풍", "겨울 선물", "길 위에서", "카운트다운", "바람개비", "파도소리", "그날 그 때", "수직과 수평", "씨 뿌리는 사람", "오 계절" 등 61권의 시집과 14권의 시선집을 출간했다. 그는 전공 분야의 교과서와 의학 정보를 일반인들에게 쉽게 전달하기 위한 실용서를 여러 권 집필했다.

　이원로 시인의 시 세계에는 생명의 근원적 주제에 대한 탐색이 담겨져 있다. 그의 작품은 과학과 의학에서 유래된 지혜와 지식을 배경으로 기민한 통찰력과 상상력을 동원하여 진실하고 아름답고 영원한 우주를 추구하고 있다. 그의 시는 순화된 색조와 우아한 운율의 언어로 예술적 동경을 수놓아 간다.

이원로 시인은 과학과 의학 전문가로서의 지성적, 감성적, 영적 경험을 바탕으로 그의 독특한 예술 세계를 개척해 가고 있다.

이 시집과 더불어 "씨 뿌리는 사람", "수직과 수평", "파도소리", 바람개비", "카운트다운", "길 위에서", "겨울 선물", "순풍", "나선 계단", "분수령", "영원의 씨", "DNA 안 은하수", "회복의 눈빛", "초대장", "밤하늘", "소생", "약속", "타임캡슐", "찻잔과 바다", "파도의 터널", "오늘 안의 내일", "우리집", "바람 소리", "꽃과 별", "빨간 열매", "파도의 터널", "우리집", "오늘 안의 내일", "바람 소리", "꽃과 별", "빨간 열매", "대화", "코로나 공황", "합창", "물결", "감사와 공감", "소리 벽화", "초점", "새벽", "장도의 서막", "타임랩스 파노라마", "전야제","나팔소리","마침 좋은 때에", "어찌 등을 미시나요", "우주유영", "불사조 행렬", "춤의 소용돌이", "진주잡이", "마중물", "섬광", "멈출 수 없는 강물", "별들의 노래", "꽃눈 나라", "피리 부는 사람", "반딧불", "울림", "시집가는 날", "시냅스", "기적은 어디에나", "화이부동", "신호추적자", "시간의 주름" 등은 아래에서 구입할 수 있다.

Amazon.com/author/leewonro와 kdp.amazon.com/bookshelf(paperbacks and e-books)